BRIGHT SHENG

THE STREAM FLOWS

For Solo Violin

ED 4088

First Printing: March 1999

G. SCHIRMER, *Inc.*

DISTRIBUTED BY

HAL•LEONARD®
CORPORATION
7777 W. BLUEMOUND RD. P.O. BOX 13819 MILWAUKEE, WI 53213

PROGRAM NOTE

The Stream Flows, which is dedicated to my teacher Hugo Weisgall, is in two parts. The first part is based on a famous folk song from the southern part of China. The freshness and richness of the tune deeply touched me when I first heard it. Since then I have used it as basic material in several of my works. Here I hope that the tone quality of a female folk singer is evoked by the timbre of the solo violin. The second part is a fast country dance based on a three-note motive.

—Bright Sheng

The Stream Flows

The rising moon shines brightly,
it reminds me of my love in the mountains.
Like the moon, you walk in the sky,
as the crystal stream flows down the mountain.

A clear breeze blows up the hill.
My love, do you hear I am calling you?

The Stream Flows *was commissioned by the*
Foundation for Chinese Performing Arts
for Nai-Yuan Hu, who gave the premiere performance
on October 20, 1990 at Jordan Hall in Boston, Massachusetts

duration: ca. 10 minutes

recording: New World Records 80407-2, Lucia Lin, violin

to Hugo Weisgall

THE STREAM FLOWS

I

Bright Sheng
(1990)

II

poco

ppp

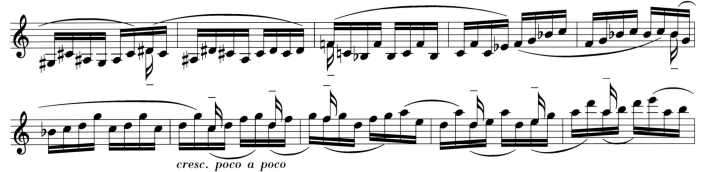

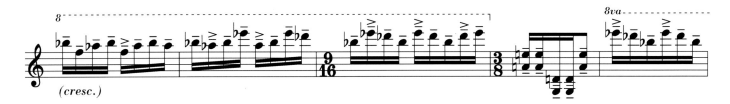